GOLDEN STATE
BATTLEWAGON
U.S.S. California (BB-44)

by Myron J. Smith, Jr.

Pictorial Histories Publishing Company
Missoula, Montana

LIBRARY OF CONGRESS CATALOG
CARD NO. 83-62228

ISBN 0-9333126-37-9

First Printing: January 1984
Second Printing: September 1987
Third Printing: March 1994
Fourth Printing: June 1999

WARSHIP SERIES
#1 Mountaineer Battlewagon, U.S.S. West Virginia (BB-48)
#2 Keystone Battlewagon, U.S.S. Pennsylvania (BB-38)
#3 Golden State Battlewagon, U.S.S. California (BB-44)

Front Cover: Artwork by James Flood

Back Cover: A 1908 postcard of the armored cruiser *California* (CA-6)

Interior Color Profiles and Line Drawings by Alan Chesley, Annapolis, Maryland

PICTORIAL HISTORIES PUBLISHING COMPANY
713 SOUTH THIRD WEST
MISSOULA, MONTANA 59801

CONTENTS

Dedication: for Dennie

INTRODUCTION

    The battleship *California* (BB-44) was the fifth, largest, and most famous ship to carry that name, though not the last. She was christened in honor of California, whose star, the 31st, came into the Union banner on September 9, 1850, less than two years after the discovery of gold at Sutter's mill brought to the former Mexican territory the great "gold rush" and the "forty-niners."

    Affectionately nicknamed "The Prune Barge," she was sometimes called the Golden State Battlewagon and was the pride of America and fleet flagship in the years before World War II. Despite a near fatal setback at Pearl Harbor, she was put back into service in time to help finish the Pacific conflict, remaining at all times a worthy symbol of the people whose spirit is exemplified in their state motto: "Eureka," or "I Have Found It."

The Screw-Sloop California.

GOLDEN STATE BATTLEWAGON
THE FIRST FOUR CALIFORNIAS

THE SCREW-SLOOP *CALIFORNIA*

The first of six naval vessels to honor the State of California was a Civil War-designed sloop-of-war launched at the Portsmouth, New Hampshire, navy yard on July 3, 1867. Originally christened the *Minnetonka*, her completion was slowed by post-war government economies. On May 15, 1869, the vessel's name was changed to *California* and she was finally commissioned on December 12, 1870, Capt. J.M.B. Clitz commanding.

Displacing 2,354 tons, the first *California* was 313 feet, 6 inches long (a little under half the length of BB-44), with a beam of 46 feet and a draft of 17 feet 2 inches. Ship-rigged with sails, as well as a coal-burning steam engine which turned a single propeller, the sloop could make 12 knots speed under the very best of conditions. Her armament of 23 guns was mixed: two 100-pound rifles, one 60-pound rifle, a pair of 20-pound rifles, and 18 smooth bore 9-inch cannon. Her complement was 325 officers and men.

The *California* reached San Francisco via the Straights of Magellan on July 30, 1871. There she became flagship of Rear Adm. John A. Winslow, whose U.S.S. *Kearsarge* had sunk the Confederate *Alabama* off Cherbourg, France, in 1864. Following a year-long cruise to Hawaii, Chile and Colombia, the sloop returned to Mare Island, where she was turned over to Rear Adm. A.M. Pennock, commanding the North Pacific Squadron and Civil War fleet captain of the Navy's Mississippi Squadron. In November 1872, Pennock took the *California* out to Hawaii once more, this time to supervise the protection of American interests in Honolulu. The ship returned to San Francisco in May 1873, where she was decommissioned. Two years later, in May 1875, the *California* was sold.

THE ARMORED CRUISER
CALIFORNIA/SAN DIEGO (ACR/CA-6)

The second *California* (ACR-6) was the last of three armored cruisers authorized by the naval building act of March 3, 1899 and the one designated to "be built on or near the coast of the Pacific Ocean." Sponsored by Miss F. Pardee, daughter of California governor George C. Pardee, the ship, sister to the *Pennsylvania* (ACR-4) and *West Virginia* (ACR-5), was launched on April 28, 1904 at the San Francisco yards of the Union Iron Works. Following a delay in the completion of her outfitting caused by the great Earthquake of 1906, the cruiser was commissioned on August 1, 1907, Capt. V.L. Cottman in command.

In a gleaming coat of white and spar color, the $3.8 million *California* displaced 13,680 tons (normal load). She was 503 feet 11 inches long with a beam of 69 feet 7 inches and a mean draught of 24 feet 1 inch. Armor on the mail belt ran 5-6 inches, depending on location, while steel protection on the turrets was 6 inches, with 9 inches on the conning tower. Her main armament consisted of four 8-inch guns in twin turrets, one forward and one aft of the superstructure. The secondary defenses featured 14 6-inch guns arranged in casemates, seven to a side, plus 18 3-inch "quick-firer" guns and two 18-inch submerged torpedo tubes. Two 3-inch anti-aircraft guns would be added in 1917. The two-shaft vertical 3-exp. reciprocating engines and BW, type WT, coal-fired boilers gave 23,000 indicated horsepower, sufficient for a seldom-achieved speed of 22 knots. Bunker space was provided for 2,075 tons of coal. Though the vessel was originally equipped with two military masts, the foremast would be removed in 1911 and replaced by a cage mast which, together with four funnels, proved the ship's most distinguishing features. Berths were provided for 47 officers and 782 enlisted men, although in the years before World War I, the ship would be lucky to have 370 volunteer bluejackets, including flag complement and Marines.

Following shakedown, Capt. Cottman's proud new vessel took part in a May 1908 San Francisco naval review. Shortly thereafter, the *California* became the flagship of Rear Adm. Giles B. Harber, commander in chief of the Pacific Fleet. That fall, she accompanied the U.S. Armored Cruiser Squadron on a short Pacific cruise to Hawaii and Samoa. The cruiser would spend much of her early career as a flagship in the Far East and Pacific, serving on those routine training and flag-showing cruises common to many American naval vessels prior to World War I.

In early 1910, the *California's* top two officers were rotated; their replacements were destined to achieve illustrious naval stature. The new captain, Capt. Henry T. Mayo, would become commander in chief of the Atlantic Fleet in 1917 while the new executive officer, Cmdr. William V. Pratt, would be named chief of naval operations in 1930. In the summer of 1910, the *California* returned to the West Coast for a year of overhaul and what seemed to her crew as never ending drills: division maneuvers, target firing, director drills and night mock attacks by torpedo boat flotillas. Incidentally, both Mayo and Pratt were transferred to other commands in early 1911.

December 1911 saw the *California* departing Mare Island for Honolulu and in March 1912, she continued westward for a brief tour on the Asiatic Station, visiting ports in China, Japan, and the Philippines. By August, she was back in San Francisco, from where she was ordered to Corinto, Nicaragua, to protect American lives and property during a time of internal political disturbances. When the Nicaraguan troubles ended, the cruiser resumed her training off the West Coast, often slipping down to Mexican waters when that nation faced internal strife.

On September 1, 1914, the *California* was renamed the *San Diego*, in order to permit assignment of the state name to the newly-authorized battleship. Thereafter, the cruiser continued her intermittent service as fleet flagship until a boiler explosion forced her into Mare Island for repair. The ship remained in "reduced commission" through the summer of 1915 after which time she resumed her flagship status until February 12, 1917, when she was placed in reserve.

The *San Diego's* reserve status lasted less than two months. Returned to full commission on April 7, 1917, she immediately began operations as flagship for Commander, Patrol Force, Pacific Fleet. On July 18, the now largely-obsolete warship was ordered, via the Panama Canal, to the East Coast—the first time that she had left the Pacific. The *San Diego* joined Cruiser Division 2 at Hampton Roads, Virginia, on August 4 and within days, began a month's duty as flagship for Commander, Cruiser Force, Atlantic Fleet.

The essential duty now set aside for the *San Diego* was to join her sister ships in

The USS California *(CA-6) enters Pearl Harbor on Dec. 18, 1911. She broke a ribbon stretched across the harbor as she passed to her mooring.* USN #NH 52436

the coastal escort of convoys through the first dangerous leg of their passages to England and France. Throughout the fall and winter and into the spring of 1918, the armored cruiser, basing at either Tompkinville, New York, or Halifax, Nova Scotia, safely conducted her charges out to meet their open-ocean escorts in the storm-ridden and submarine-infested North Atlantic. During those months, she put in a single overseas trip, to LaCrosie, France, in November 1917.

In April 1918, the German admiralty elected to launch a concentrated campaign against U.S. shipping in American waters. Consequently, it ordered seven of its largest U-boats, including four of the converted *Deutschland*-class mercantile submarines, to ply Yankee waters at staggered 5-6 week intervals between mid-April and late August. Employing torpedoes, gunfire and, more importantly, mines laid in random fields, these enemy boats harrassed coastal shipping and disturbed the convoy people in the Navy Department, although the effort would actually have no lasting impact on the American war effort.

One of the U-boats sent to operate off the East Coast during this German offen-sive was the converted *Deutschland*-class giant *U-156*. Among the locations her skipper chose to drop his many mines were the shipping lanes along Fire Island, on the Atlantic side of Long Island. There, southeast of Sandy Hook off the Fire Island light, the *San Diego*, enroute to New York from Portsmouth, New Hampshire, hit one of the mines on July 19, 1918. Although the cruiser sank only 28 minutes after the great explosion rocked her hull, only six crewmen died; 1,183 survivors were quickly picked up and removed to safety.

The *San Diego*, representative of the Golden State for over ten years, was gone, the largest U.S. warship lost to enemy action during the First World War. Perhaps it would have comforted the widows and friends of her dead sailors to know that, within two months, the U-boat that had sown the mine that claimed the *San Diego* would also be sunk—ironically by an American mine. Returning to Germany at the end of September, the 1,512-ton, 213-foot *U-156* struck a U.S. Navy mine while attempting a passage through the North Sea Mine Barrage and sank. Only 26 men survived.

Aerial view of the armored cruiser prior to 1914; note cage mast (right) and awning over stern (left).   USN #NH67711

USS San Diego *(CA-6), formerly the* California, *is shown sinking off Long Island, New York, on July 19, 1918, after hitting a mine laid by a German U-Boat. Painting by Francis Muller, 1920.*

USN #NH55012

THE LARGE CONVERTED-YACHT
CALIFORNIA/HAUOLI (SP-249)

In response to the demand of a rich patron, Clara B. Stocker, the Brooklyn firm of Robbins Drydock Company built a steam yacht in 1903. This elaborately-appointed vessel displaced 299 tons, was 211 feet long, with a 22-foot beam and an 8-foot draft, and on trials proved herself a fast steamer at 19 knots. Mrs. Stocker, well pleased with her new acquisition, christened it *Hauoli*, the Hawaiian word for delight. The yacht was employed for parties and pleasure cruises and sometime before 1917 its name, for an unknown reason was changed to *California*.

When America joined World War I, the Navy found itself with a pressing need for escort, patrol, and dispatch vessels. Learning that Mrs. Stocker was willing to sell, fleet representatives purchased the yacht in August 1917, taking her into the Navy as the third *California* the same month the former *California*, now *San Diego*, arrived in Virginia. Outfitted at the New York Navy Yard, the yacht was converted into a patrol vessel; she was painted gray and armed with two 6-pound cannon and a pair of Colt machine guns. The new *California* was designated SP-249 and commissioned the day before Christmas, Lt. j.g. W. Applebye-Robinson, U.S. Naval Reserve Force, commanding.

The *California's* first year was passed as a patrol vessel in New York harbor. There word reached her on February 18, 1918, that somebody in Washington had noted the state name of California was reserved and she would have to be rechristened; accordingly, SP-249 once more became the *Hauoli*. Her wartime service occasionally took her outside the harbor transporting passengers to and from convoys, but all-in-all, her World War I operations were routine and without incident.

On January 28, 1919, the *Hauoli* was transferred to special duty and began her most significant service. For the next seven months, she was assigned to the experimental use of Thomas A. Edison. The famous inventor was then engaged in a series of anti-submarine warfare experiments; listening devices of his design were installed in *Hauoli* and tested in and around New York harbor. Before demobilization cut short the experiments with the gunboat, she was withdrawn from Edison and decommissioned on October 8, 1919. On September 7, 1920, the little warship was sold to the Denton Shore Lumber Company of Tampa, Florida.

THE SMALL CONVERTED-YACHT
CALIFORNIA (SP-647)

The fourth *California* was also a steam yacht, built in San Francisco in 1910. Sometime before 1917, the 84-ton, 58-foot vessel, which could make 9.2 knots full throttle, passed into the hands of the San Francisco Bar Pilot's Association. She was loaned to the Navy on the outbreak of war and was commissioned as SP-647. This *California* served on local patrol until she was returned to her owners at the end of 1918.

Motor Boat California *prior to World War I. She was commissioned as SP-647 at the outbreak of the war.* USN #NH 83803

USS California *(BB-44) still under construction Nov. 22, 1919, at Mare Island Navy Yard, following her launching ceremony two days earlier.*
USN #NH69031

CREATION

The General Board, that senior U.S. Navy council which set the characteristics to which all American warships were designed between 1910 and 1945, laid great importance on the ability of pre-World War II battleships to operate together as a fleet, especially in the Pacific. This view was operationally held by all Navy leaders from the chief of naval operations downwards. As far as possible, these people insisted that successive designs be given similar speeds, radii of action, and handling/survivability qualities. This orderly process was not lost on U.S. lawmakers, who continuously specified in their battlewagon authorization acts that new ships carry "as heavy armor and as powerful armaments as any vessel of their class." Indeed, the General Board always advocated dreadnoughts which would equal or outclass the latest of Britain, Germany, or Japan.

The General Board characteristics drawn up in 1910 called for oil-burning battleships which featured "all-or-nothing armor," i.e., heavy steel along the waterline and over vital areas and little medium-weight protection, machinery for 21 knots, and a dozen 14-inch rifles in triple turrets. On March 3, 1915, with World War I then seven months old and Japan restless in the Pacific, Congress authorized President Woodrow Wilson to acquire two more battleships in addition to the three of the

New Mexico class allowed the previous year. Whatever came, American leaders would have the Navy, the nation's first line of defense, ready.

Authorized as Battleship No. 44, the *California*, and her sister the *Tennessee* (No. 43), were, with only minor changes, a duplication of the three *New Mexicos. Jane's Fighting Ships* called their design "practically identical." Congress, in allowing the pair, had specified that neither exceed a delivery cost of $7.8 million, less armor and armament. Total cost for the ship was $12.75 million. While that still seems like a lot of money—and in 1915 dollars it was—these ultimates in strategic weaponry for their day were each completed for slightly over 45 percent of the 1981 projected cost of reactivating the World War II *New Jersey* (BB-62) for service with today's fleet. Indeed, BB-44's cost would be only 25.64 percent of the $200 million price of her successor, GCN-36.

Calling her "the most powerful battleship in the world," officials of the Bureau of Construction and Repair on October 28, 1915 assigned the task of building the *California* to the Mare Island Navy Yard in Vallejo, California. There the keel was laid on October 25, 1916, a few days short of six months following the Battle of Jutland. The first frames were up within weeks, and as inspectors checked the progress through 1916-1919, thousands of builders, when not building more urgently re-

The battleship just after launching at Mare Island, Nov. 20, 1919.

USN # NH 55020

11

quired escorts and merchantmen, worked on the hull. As the time of launch approached, the craft, its hull and decks in place, was nearly 55 percent complete.

The christening of the *California* was set for November 20, 1919, just over a year after the Armistice ended the war. In the ancient ceremony, the sponsor, Mrs. Barbara Stephens Zane, daughter of California Governor William D. Stephens, surrounded by prominent Navy and civilian officials including her father, smashed the traditional champagne bottle across the bow. This signal sent the ship sliding down greased ways into San Pablo Bay. The huge vessel's outfitting would continue apace for two and a half more years as the main belt armor was installed, the turrets built and guns installed, and the superstructure completed, including provisions for her already-determined role as a fleet flagship. Finally, early on a warm August 10, 1921, the sparkling new battleship, her brass polished and gray paint still fresh in places, was ready to join the Navy.

Just after noon that sunny August day, the remainder of the ship's 57 officers, 70 Marines, and 1,026 bluejackets came aboard and, after stowing their gear, assembled at divisional parade on the quarterdeck aft. The national ensign was hoisted at the flag staff, the commission pennant was broken out at the main truck, and a band played the "Star Spangled Banner." The commandant of the Mare Island yard then turned the ship over to Capt. Henry J. Ziegemeier, who in turn read aloud his orders and a salutatory telegram from Gov. Stephens. Following a short address to the crew of his new command, the skipper ordered the first watch set. Divisions were marched forward and within an hour the *California* was opened to a throng of visitors.

Christening ceremonies for the USS California *on Nov. 20, 1919, by Mrs. Barbara Stephens Zane, daughter of California Governor William D. Stephens.*

USN #NH 70524

PHYSICAL APPEARANCE

A capital ship like the *California* had a long sweeping top deck, covered with teak which enlisted men were expected to "swab" (scrub) white, and a raised "fo'c'sle" for the half length forward. Out of these rose the masts and funnels, the topside bridgework, and other structures collectively known as the superstructure. From the main deck, too, rose the bulky main turrets, holding the 14-inch guns. Each was mounted on top of roller-path bearings within a fixed armored tube called a barbette. The hull, with its distinctive clipper bow, was very similar to that of the *New Mexicos*, although there were no recesses for casemates as the 5-inchers were spotted strategically in "dry" positions at upper deck level. Other features included the introduction of turbo-electric drive, the improvement of underwater protection, more elaborate bridgework, and the return to twin funnels. Displacing 32,600 (normal) or 35,190 tons (full load), the new dreadnought had an overall length of 624 feet 6 inches (600 feet at the waterline), a beam of 97 feet 4 inches, and a mean draught of 30 feet 6 inches, which could be extended to a maximum draught of 35 feet 6 inches. In layman's terms, the *California* was a bit longer than two football fields and as tall as an eight-story building.

The *California*, like the *Tennessee* and the succeeding three units of the *Colorado*-class, was known as an electric-drive ship. The main power plant consisted of eight electrically-controlled, oil-burning Bureau Express boilers with a combined total heating surface of 50,984 square feet, exhaust from which rose through flue gas ducts to the two slim funnels directly overhead. Located in separate watertight compartments (four to port and four to starboard) under central control abeam the engine room, these boilers produced the steam which, in turn, powered a pair of large General Electric turbo-electric geared turbines, arranged in tandem on the centerline. Controlled by mechanical governors from one small room, the two three-phase, 15,000 kva main generators (coupled to the turbines) sent a total of 6,800 volts to the ship's four 4,300 kw alternating-current motors, each of which was attached to a single propeller shaft. The total estimated weight of all this machinery was 1,805 tons.

The electric motors of BB-44 were designed for 24 and 36 poles and featured squirrel-cage winding for starting and wound-rotor for running. At 170 rpm (0.98pf), each motor developed 6,800 hp. The 1921 battlewagon gave a total designated shaft horsepower of 28,500 (compared with the 1920 destroyer *Pruitt's* [DD-347] 27,500), sufficient for Capt. Ziegemeier's best trial run of 21.46 knots. The *California's* normal fuel-oil capacity was 2,200 tons (over 600,000 gallons) with a maximum of 3,328 tons, enough for an approximate range of up to 4,000 miles. Fuel consumption, at 17 knots, was 1.07 lb./s.h.p. The ship's tactical diameter (turning radius), with screws turning forward and full helm, was 700 yards. Course direction was controlled via a single rudder.

The arrangement, thickness, and extent of the *California's* armor was basically similar to that of the *New Mexicos*, although the layout was somewhat modified and underwater protection was significantly improved, her hull, and that of her sister,

Fitting out at Mare Island Navy Yard, 1920.　　　USN #NH 55021

being the first built to a "post-Jutland" design. A waterline belt of 14-inch steel was designed to effectively resist the penetration of a 14-inch shell fired from 14,000 yards. Extending 9 feet above the waterline and 8½ feet below, this belt—thickest abreast the turret magazines and amidships machinery spaces—tapered to 8 inches toward the ends (and at its lower edge), closing with transverse armored bulkheads. Designers, continuing the "all-or-nothing" protection concept begun with the *Nevada* (BB-36), agreed that, given stability requirements, thick armor could not also be placed over the top deck. Instead, they would continue to minimize the effects of "plunging fire" by providing BB-44 with enough cover to absorb fragments from exploding shells. The deck armor extended over the machinery areas and steering gear; the outboard strakes of the upper deck were covered with 1½ inches, the main deck amidships by 3½ inches, and the outboard strakes of the lower deck by 1½-2 inches. To prevent flue gasses from filling the ship in battle, the boiler uptakes received 15 inches of steel at the funnel bases, tapering to 8 inches at the upper deck.

To aid in torpedo protection, the *California* featured a 17-foot protective layer inboard of her belt. This layer was divided on each side of the hull by three unpierced longitudinal bulkheads, each covered by ¼-inch steel plate. The large outer bulkhead was divided into five compartments inside the ship's skin, of which the three center ones were filled with fuel oil while the two outer ones were left as air spaces. Theoretically, the skin would cause an incoming "tin fish" to explode and rupture. The compressed air in the first void would tend to absorb the expanding gasses vented into the ship by the explosion and distribute their force against bulkhead No. 1. The oil in three center compartments would, according to the design, take up much of the shock by its inertia and, by its incompressibility, cause bulkheads 2, 3 and 4 to help withstand the shock simultaneously, with bulkhead 1. Compartment E was left as a compressible void so that bulkhead No. 5 would not share in withstanding the major shock, but serve as a flooding boundary in case bulkheads 2, 3, and 4 were ruptured. The oil in the center compartments, incidentally, was a part of the dreadnought's fuel, but could be replaced by water as it was consumed.

Some felt that water would serve even better than oil in the ship's center compartments as it could absorb more of an explosion's terrific heat, thus reducing its intensity. At Pearl Harbor, the oil arrangement worked well as the chief salvage officer, Capt. Homer N. Wallin, testified: "The two torpedo hits...were the most serious damage sustained.... In each case the inboard bulkhead was practically intact.... *California* was well designed...entirely able to withstand the punishment received on 7 December."

Elsewhere, the main battery was also well covered. The face of each 14-inch turret received 18 inches of steel while the sides and rear had 8 inches and the roof 5 inches. The 411 tons of barbette armor for each 1,127-ton turret was reduced in thickness as it descended behind the main belt, running 14 inches on the exposed sides, 16 inches on the tube, and 14 inches on the crown. Protection for the conning tower, from which the ship would be controlled in a surface gunnery action, and the main armament directors, was 16 inches thick, but was much reduced for the high-angle directors.

The *California's* main armament—her reason for being—consisted of a dozen

USS California *(BB-44), circa 1921, at speed.*   USN #NH55026

14

separately sleeved 14-inch/50 caliber 81.7-ton guns mounted in superfiring triple turrets, two forward and two aft. Each of these rifled guns, some 46 inches in diameter at the breech, had a maximum 30° elevation and could fire a 1,500-lb. armor-piercing (AP) shell to the 34,000-35,000 yard range (approximately 19-20 miles) at an average rate of fire of 1.5 per minute!

The battleship's secondary armament (changed several times before the attack at Pearl Harbor) initially comprised fourteen 5-inch/51 caliber single-purpose "anti-destroyer" guns distributed seven to a side. Four were in open top deck mounts, 2 forward and 2 aft between the funnels, with ten in second deck casemates. Additionally, four semi-automatic 3-inch/50 caliber guns were carried for anti-aircraft protection, as well as a battery of saluting cannon, a field piece of amphibious exercises, various machine guns and small arms. In 1922, the two 5-inchers located between the funnels were removed and four more 3-inch anti-aircraft pieces were added. All of the anti-aircraft guns were replaced in 1929-30 by eight 5-inch/25 caliber guns while in 1936, anti-aircraft protection was augmented by the receipt of additional light machine guns. A pair of submerged 21-inch torpedo tubes aboard on commissioning day were found unworkable and were removed in 1937.

Stern view of the battleship, circa 1921. Note "range clock" on main mast and "bearing scales" on No. 3 turret.
USN #NH55023

As built, the *California* sported a pair of 140-foot lattice, or "cage," masts which supported large fire control, or "fighting," tops. With a large diameter at the base providing support, each mast was formed from two inclined sets of steel tubing (clamped together at intersections) which made up rigidity-assuring sets of triangles. The enclosed mast tops housed the main and secondary control stations, the latter one level below the former. Complementing the main battery rangefinder atop the bridge, one was placed on a mainmast platform in 1927 while the secondary directors continued in their platform locations, one on either side of the lower level of the tops. In support of communications gear, each mast also featured large yardarms and hinged topmasts with small yardarms. A platform encircling the main mast carried four large searchlights. Range clocks were also carried fore and aft of the lower levels of the tops (one facing the bow and one the stern) which could be used by admirals with, or independently of, the bearing scales painted on the sides of turrets II and III to mass fire (in poor visibility or smoke) for devastating effect. These two masts were the ship's most distinguishing pre-war characteristics and as they were also fitted aboard her sister and the *Colorados*, distinguished them from the rest of the battleship force as members of the "Big Five."

In 1929/30, an aircraft catapult was fitted on the fantail, serviced by a simple derrick (later replaced by a crane). Another catapult was fitted atop turret III to be serviced by the cranes which also handled cargo and the small boats/barges stacked amidships. The three aircraft carried would vary in type, but were always stowed atop the catapults.

Following the Washington Treaty of 1922, the U.S. Navy, with the limited peacetime funding available, began the reconstruction of its active battleships, the more elderly first. Funds for the modernization of the *California* and *Tennessee* were authorized in April 1939, but in view of the situations in Europe and the Far East, it was decided to hold off their rebuilding. With minor improvements, the two ships would be held in a state of readiness in case war threatened.

When on October 20, 1942, the *California* arrived at the Puget Sound Navy Yard at Bremerton, Washington, from Pearl Harbor, she appeared somewhat similar to her pre-December 7 silhouette, even though her cage masts and catapults were gone. At Bremerton, the ship would undergo permanent repairs to damages suffered in the Japanese raid and would be completely and thoroughly modernized. So extensive was her outward transformation to be that she would become practically a new ship. Due to higher priorities, however, this rebuilding was often interrupted and finally set back by several months.

Steel-helmeted yard workers cut the ship clean of superstructure and secondary guns, stripping her completely down to second deck level. With only the original

Off New York City, May 1934.   NA #80-G-1021358

Under way in San Francisco Bay, late 1930s.   USN #1021941

hull, main battery, and propulsion plant retained, her almost total conversion was begun practically from scratch. As opposed to the riveting employed in her creation, the *California's* new work was all welded, bringing a weight savings which allowed other improvements. Apart from selected new horizontal deck armor doubled in thickness, her hull received deep 8-foot 3-inch bulges on both sides, which gradually tapered toward bow and stern. These "blisters" formed a kind of "second hull," covering the entire side armor from below the waterline to the upper deck, providing increased stability and better anti-torpedo protection. Internal compartmentation was rearranged and improved; new fire mains, 154 miles of new electric cable, a new ventilation system and new fuel lines were added while fuel storage capacity was extended. The hull construction, by the way, widened the dreadnought's beam to 114 feet, a girth which would prevent her from ever passing through the Panama Canal again.

The most striking innovation was made in the battleship's superstructure. The heavy armored conning tower, stacks, etc. were all removed. A compact superstructure of standard design was built, able to provide essential ship and gunnery control facilities while offering as little interference as possible in the fields of fire of the ship's now-essential anti-aircraft guns. A low tower foremast supported a main battery director and bridges; boiler uptakes were trunked into a single stack which was faired into the afterside of the foremast, the whole forming a compact block. A low structure was set just abaft the stack in the location once occupied by the after cage mast to accommodate the after 14-inch director. These changes gave the old lady a look similar to the newer battleships of the *South Dakota* class.

Before Bremerton, the *California* wore navy-gray #3 paint. In order to disguise her somewhat for Japanese sea and airborne marksmen, she was now given one of the Navy's standard camouflage schemes, or "measures," which at range and in various weather and lighting conditions would change her profile. The measure chosen for the *California* was No. 32, the "medium pattern system." Under this arrangement, she was painted in dazzle-pattern with pale gray, haze gray, and navy blue applied to horizonal surfaces and decks. The ship's identification numbers were painted on the hull fore and aft, but were purposely made very small.

Based on war experience, the Navy insisted that the *California's* secondary and anti-aircraft armament be substantially increased from what it had been previously. Accordingly, the casemated 5-inch/51's, and the 5-inch/25's were replaced by sixteen 5-inch/38 caliber superfiring dual purpose guns in eight twin mounts, four to a side on the "02" deck. For close-in anti-aircraft defense fourteen quadruple 40mm Bofors mounts and 52 20mm Oerlikon machine guns were fitted, including three atop turret no. 3.

Fleet Adm. Chester W. Nimitz served as a member of the staff of Commander in Chief, Battle Fleet, from June 1923 to October 1925.   USN #NH 58113

Painting the waterline in drydock, 1938.   USN #NH 80520

Gunnery control and radar equipment were modernized and/or initially installed. Two Mark (MK) 34 main battery directors, with MK 8 fire control radars and assorted gunfire computing equipment, were placed aboard while four "FD" instruments were arranged around the superstructure for the 5-inchers. In addition, a type "SK-2" radar aerial was mounted on the forward pole mast while an "SP" antenna was attached to the tall main mast. These mechanical eyes of the *California* gave her scanning capability to 60,000 yards, precision ranging to 44,000 yards, and the ability to "shoot at night almost as well as by day."

Finally, the prewar catapults on turret III, or the "high" catapult and the fantail,

which were removed at Pearl Harbor, were replaced by a single catapult on the fantail, serviced by a crane. The *California* received four new Vought OS2U "Kingfisher" observation aircraft, sometimes affectionately known as the ship's "Quarterdeck Messerschmidts." Rebuilt, reconditioned, and bearing no resemblance to her former self, the battleship stood out of the yard at the end of January 1944. Following a series of "in and out" sea trials and exercises off San Pedro and a final Bremerton check of her machinery, the *California* arrived in Hawaii in mid-May, ready to go to war.

Flagship of the U.S. Navy Battle Force off San Pedro, Calif., in the 1930s.

NA #80-G-1021343

Bow view off of San Pedro, Calif., 1930s. NA #80-G-1021350

Docked at Balboa, Canal Zone, 1930s. NA #80-G-1921350

19

Vought 03U Corsair being hoisted aboard, 1930s.
USN #NH 80521

Liberty party prepares to go ashore in 1940. Note large letters "Cal" on boat stowed aboard forward of the funnel. Also note the Curtiss SOC-3 Seagull seaplane with dark fuselage. This was the "flag plane" of the Commander, Battle Force, U.S. Fleet.
USN #80516

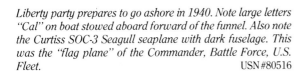

OPERATIONAL HISTORY, THROUGH PEARL HARBOR, 1921-1941

Subsequent to commissioning, offical trials, and shakedown training, the *California* was made flagship of the Battleship Force, Pacific Fleet. In 1922 the Pacific Fleet was redesignated the Battle Fleet (renamed the Battle Force in 1931), United States Fleet. For the next two decades, the battleship divisions of the Battle Fleet/Battle Force were to include the preponderance of the Navy's strength and for most of those years, the *California* continued her flagship duty.

Peacetime service involved an annual cycle of maintenance, training, and readiness exercises. Each year, the great gray vessels took part in competitions in engineering performance and gunnery as well as an annual fleet problem (war game). Beginning with Fleet Problem I in 1923 and continuing through Fleet Problem XXI in April 1940, the flagship, naturally, held a prominent position in these battle exercises. Meanwhile, her individual proficiency was immediately shown. The prized Battle Efficiency Pennant, the "Meatball," was hoisted aboard in 1921-1922 in recognition of the ship's having the highest combined total score in gunnery and engineering competition. During the competitive year 1925-1926, the *California* had the highest aggregate score in the list of record practices fired by her guns of various caliber and won the Gunnery "E," for excellence. From July to September 1925, she led the Battle Fleet and a squadron of light cruisers on a successful good-will tour to Australia and New Zealand. In 1927, 1930, and 1934, the Golden State namesake participated in Presidential fleet reviews.

Throughout the 1930's, in the Pacific and occasionally the Atlantic, the *California* continued her training and flagship mission. Exercises were met and dignitaries were received on board, including admirals changing their commands. Cities along the American coast celebrating centennials or other festivals often found the great dreadnought holding open house in their ports. Somewhere along the line in those years, fleet bluejackets came to nickname her the "Prune Barge," because, wrote Adm. Wallin years later, "that state produced a large quantity of prunes for export." Complimentary or not, suitable or not, the sobriquet would stick throughout the remainder of the *California's* career.

Fleet Problem XXI was conducted in Hawaiian waters during the spring of 1940. At the end of the exercise, the Battle Force did not, as was its practice, return to San Pedro. In hopes that a strong signal might deter Japanese Far Eastern expansion, President Roosevelt, over the objections of CINCUS Adm. James O. Richardson (shortly thereafter relieved by Adm. Husband E. Kimmel), ordered his battleships to remain based at Pearl Harbor that summer. The following spring, the *California* was overhauled at Puget Sound and after a week of liberty for the crew in San Francisco, departed the West Coast once again on April 15, 1941.

From late 1940 to December 7, 1941, the "Prune Barge," with time out for two trips to California (the last in October '41), carried out a schedule of training, basing on Pearl Harbor, steaming with various task forces and groups in the Hawaiian operating area. Commanded by Capt. Joel W. Bunkley and flying the flag of Commander, Battle Force, Vice Adm. William S. Pye, the dreadnought led a number of two-week evolutions at sea, each followed by a week in port for upkeep. These exercises were executed under combat conditions. Battle stations were maintained watch-on-watch as evasive actions were practiced for simulated enemy attack. Gunnery, damage control, and fire drills were constant. The last of Pye's cruises occurred during the first week of December 1941; at its conclusion, the overdue battlewagons put into Pearl Harbor, maneuvering up around Ford Island and down to the southeast side to a series of masonry mooring quays often known as "battleship row."

Japanese secret agent Takeo Yoshikawa reported the units of the Battle Force late on December 6. Torpedo nets, he noted, were not spread and aerial surveillance

Exercises on deck, March 4, 1923.   USN #NH55029

had been nil. The *California* lay moored at Quay F-3, the row's southernmost, with some 40-60 feet of water under her keel. Like her sisters astern, she lay in Readiness Condition Three (or "X")—two machine guns manned and two 5-inch guns prepared with ready ammunition and crews. Fuel and food were onboard and the engine room was on twelve-hour notice. It being a weekend, many of her officers and men, including Capt. Bunkley, Adm. Pye, and the executive officer, Cmdr. Earl E. Stone, were on liberty ashore. Those left onboard played cards, napped, or read under the watchful eye of the capable Lt. Cmdr. M.N. Little, the ship's first lieutenant and acting commander.

"It is a well-known fact, although never admitted, that battleships carrying admirals' flags," wrote Samuel Eliot Morison in the first volume of his semi-official history, "although taut and smart in appearance, were commonly inferior to others in readiness and material condition." Such was the case aboard the *California*: "her material condition as to watertight integrity was bad." According to a variety of experts, the "Prune Barge" would be lost, as Bureau of Ships War Damage Report No. 21 of November 28, 1942 has it, because "manholes (on the double bottom) left open...and loose manhole covers on the port side of the third deck and because most of the watertight fittings on the third deck and below were open...." Why watertight integrity was so poor remains controversial.

In his January 26, 1942 after-action report, Capt. Bunkley stated that a material inspection of the *California* was imminent and normal preparations required a thorough venting of tanks and voids. This view, reported and repeated by Morison and others as recently as Dr. Gordon W. Prange in his massive *At Dawn We Slept*, may not be accurate. The 1946 Joint Congressional Committee on the Investigation of the Pearl Harbor Attack examined the manhole/inspection question closely. A schedule of major inspections noted on p. 1677 of its *Hearings* does not list the "Prune Barge." A statement on p. 5351 ends, "...the logs of the U.S.S. *California, Maryland, Nevada,* and *Tennessee* have been examined for any record of inspections, and for any references concerning watertight integrity precedent to or in preparation for any inspections on 5, 6, and 7 December 1941, with negative results." The Bureau of Ships never learned for certain how many manhole covers were off or loose at the time of the Japanese raid and evidence provided by the captain varies substantially from that found during salvage operations. Whatever the exact number and the reason for them, this weakening of the ship's defenses, even if regarded as a minor oversight, would turn out to be a serious matter—one so serious that it meant the difference between the *California's* survival and her loss.

Just before 0800 on December 7, warplanes from the six carriers of Vice Adm. Chuichi Nagumo's First Air Fleet commenced their well-planned attack. Shortly thereafter, radios were calling in plain English: "Air Raid Pearl Harbor—This is No Drill!"

Immediately after the attack alarm sounded aboard the *California*, but before the maximum degree of watertight integrity could be set, even so far as the ship's bad material condition would permit, the Japanese were on her. About 0805 as the ready machine guns opened fire on planes attacking up the line, a low-flying Nakajima B5N "Kate" approached from the direction of Merry Point, banked steeply, and launched a torpedo. With a clearly-visible bubble track, the "fish" sped into the

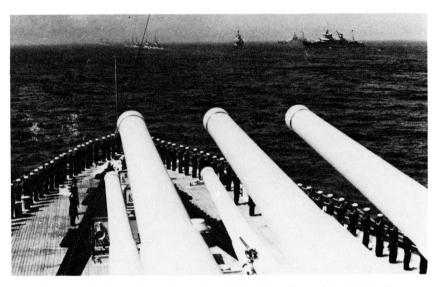

Crew manning the rails at a fleet review, 1938. Other ships included, USS Indianapolis *(CA-35),* USS Pennsylvania *(BB-38) and* USS Houston *(CA-30), plus some flush-decked destroyers to left of center.* USN #NH 80526

Firing 5"/51 Cal. guns in night battle exercise, 1923. Note 14-inch guns at right. USN #NH 55030

Pre-war aerial view of the USS California *(BB-44).*

The *California* as outfitted late in 1941.

Measure One Camouflage System: All vertical surfaces from top of boot-topping to tops of funnels were painted dark gray (5-D) (This is not ocean gray [5-0]). All vertical surface above tops of stacks were painted light gray (5-L). All horizontal surfaces (except wood decking—which was left natural) were painted dark gray (5-D).

USS CALIFORNIA (BB–

The *California* as outfitted in April of 1945.

Measure 21 Camouflage System: All vertical surfaces, from boot-topping to tops of masts, were painted navy blue (5-N). All horizontal surfaces (including all wood decking) were painted deck blue (20-B).

USS CALIFORNIA (BB–

1941

1945

Note: Colors in both renderings are toned down so that detail will not be obscured. Reference for camouflage schemes came from book on the subject by Larry Sowinsk and Thomas Walkowiak.

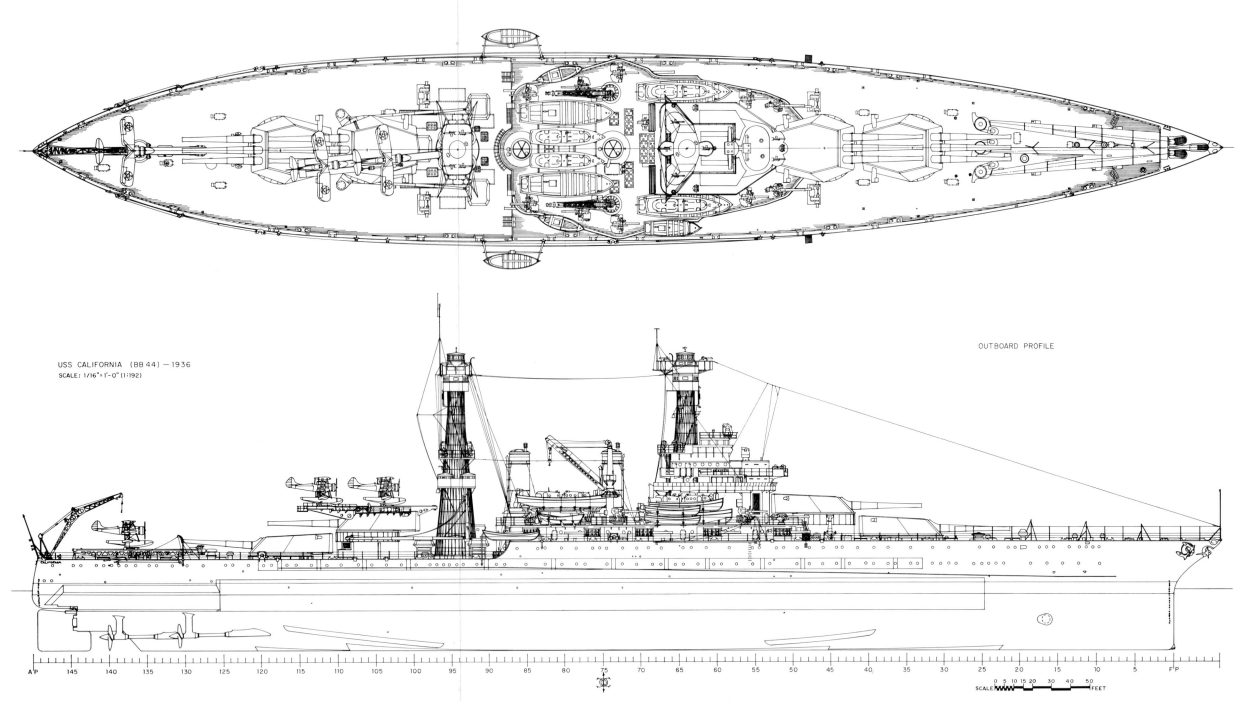

USS CALIFORNIA (BB 44) — 1936   OVERHEAD VIEW

OUTBOARD PROFILE

USS CALIFORNIA (BB 44) — 1936
SCALE: 1/16"= 1'-0" (1:192)

A'P   145   140   135   130   125   120   115   110   105   100   95   90   85   80   75   70   65   60   55   50   45   40   35   30   25   20   15   10   5   F'P

SCALE   0 5 10 15 20   30   40   50   FEET

Drawings by Alan Chesley. Copyright © 1983 Pictorial Histories Publishing Co.

port beam below the armor belt at frame 101 (turret III), lifting a heavy column of water alongside with the force of the explosion. The seaplane tender *Avocet* (AVP-4) moored at the NAS Dock, Ford Island, took the plane under fire with her two 3-inchers; the "Kate" burst into flames and crashed adjacent to the Naval Hospital. Simultaneously, a second torpedo hit the port side, again below the armor belt, at frame 52 (between turret II and the bridge).

Due to the "unbuttoned" condition of the "Prune Barge," the two torpedo hits "proved to be far-reaching and disastrous." Although neither hit punched completely through the ship's "well-designed" torpedo bulkheads, their wallop began a port list which, but for prompt counterflooding by Reserve Ensign Edgar M. Fain, might have capsized her. The forward torpedo, which ripped open a 24 by 10 foot hole, allowed salt water to contaminate the fuel lines; before they could be cleared, all power and light was lost. Meanwhile, Lt. Little was everywhere, encouraging the men and issuing emergency orders. The anti-aircraft guns were firing with ammunition brought up by hand. Toward 0825, Cmdr. Stone appeared on the bridge, the first of the *California's* top officers to get back. Adm. Pye, though not tactically in control of the ship, was speeding toward the dock with the manager of a local hotel while Capt. Bunkley, caught by the raid in swim trunks near the pool of the Halekulani, was also enroute.

Just as Stone and Little were conferring on the torpedo hits, Japanese "Val" dive bombers and several "Zero" fighters turned their attention to the flagship. After a stick of bombs dropped alongside, a huge 250 kilogram missile hit the starboard upper deck level at frame 60 and passed through to explode on the armored second deck, setting off an anti-aircraft ammunition magazine, killing 53 men. A second bomb ruptured the bow plates while near-misses caused fragmentation damage to the funnels and starboard anti-aircraft batteries. Strafing wounded a number of crewmen.

Smoke from the bomb which blew the ammunition locker infiltrated the second and third decks. Acrid fumes found their way into the forward engine room, via the ventilation system, delaying efforts there to clear the fuel lines of water from the torpedo hit. Nevertheless, tremendous efforts by damage control parties restored light and power and controlled several fires by the time Capt. Bunkley returned aboard. However, before he could issue orders to unmoor and get under way on the four available boilers, another crisis erupted.

Around 1000, burning oil from other ships drifting down the harbor engulfed the *California's* stern. Bunkley ordered "Abandon Ship," but within 15 minutes, the wind blew the burning oil pool clear. The skipper ordered all hands to return on board, but not all would and those who did, did so slowly. After witnessing an officer on shore begging a group of men, yeoman Durrell Conner, still aboard, had an idea which helped. Noting that the national ensign had yet to be raised this day, he and another seaman hoisted the colors on the fantail. A cheer went up from the men on shore and soon many were hurrying back. Unfortunately, by this time the situation was beyond repair.

Although gas powered pumps were borrowed from other ships and the minesweepers *Bobolink* (AM-20) and *Vireo* (AM-52) came alongside to apply their pumps, the *California* was sinking slowly. Even though the fires were put out, there was now no watertight integrity below the second deck. Flooding caused "by a com-

Boxing match during fleet maneuvers off Panama, 1923.   USN (All Hands)

Ship's orchestra under the guns of #4 turret, 1939. Note State of California "Bear" emblem on music stands.   USN #NH 80827

23

bination of battle damage, non-closure of watertight fittings, and rupture of ventilation ducts," could not be halted. Thus the effort to stop the sea water entering her great gashes amounted to "simply pumping Pearl Harbor through the ship."

Despite three days of attempts to save her, the *California*, though partially afloat, continued to settle. "Adequate pumping," wrote her salvage supervisor in 1968, "if it could have been supplied at the time, would have kept the vessel afloat." Neither the giant pumps required nor sufficient divers were available for the task and late on Wednesday night, December 10, the battleship came to rest in about 16 feet of soft mud. With a list to port of some 5½ degrees and a draft of about 43 feet forward and 57 feet aft, only her masts and superstructure rose above the waves. As observers noted Thursday morning, the sea had closed over the port side forward and over turret IV on the quarterdeck. Of the 120 officers and 1,546 men aboard on December 7, 6 officers and 92 men were killed or missing with another 3 officers and 58 men wounded. After two happy decades of "smooth sailing," Pearl Harbor marked a sudden and bitter end for the Golden State Battlewagon.

Top: Scrubbing canvas, 1938.   USN #NH 55031

Bottom left: Interior view of crew's messing spaces, showing mess tables with a variety of dishes, 1938.   USN #NH 80831

Bottom right: Scene in the ship's bake shop, 1931.   USN #NH 55031

The California *burning at her mooring across from Ford Island on Dec. 7, 1941.*

The "basket" mainmast was removed from the battleship in February 1942, during the Pearl Harbor salvage operation. USN #NH 55038

U.S.S. CALIFORNIA   9 APRIL 1942
VIEW FROM THE DRYDOCK CAISSON JUST AS THE
DOCK BECAME DRY. NOTE THE MUD ON PROPELLOR
SHAFTS AND STRUTS.   # 565-42

U.S.S. CALIF....
COFFERDAM ON ....
BOW, C.... OF ....

Refloating operation, March 30, 1942.   USN #NH 55036

View of ship on April 9, 1942, from the drydock caisson just as the dock became dry.
Note the mud on the propeller shafts and struts, Pearl Harbor Ship Yard.
USN #NH 64483

26

Top: Torpedo hole in the hull of the battleship. Photo taken after she had been raised and drydocked. Note armor belt above the hole. WA #80-G-32917

Bottom left: Photo taken off the port quarter shows the ship after being raised from the bottom of Pearl Harbor. The wooden structure around the after end is the coffer-dam construction to hold out water while the ship was being raised, March 1942.
USN (All Hands)

Bottom right: Battleship being towed to drydock at Pearl Harbor, April 1942.
USN (All Hands)

Top: View off port bow as the California *leaves the drydock, June 7, 1942.*   USN

Bottom left: *Removing one of the 14-inch guns from the* California.   USN (All Hands)

Bottom right: *Looking down on reconstruction of #1 and #2 14-inch turrets, Pearl Harbor, 1942.*   NA #80-G-10028

Stern view at the Pearl Harbor dock, August 1942. She left under her own power on Oct. 10, 1942, for repairs on the West Coast.

NA #80-G-10031

OPERATIONAL HISTORY, FROM SALVAGE TO DECOMMISSION, 1942-1947

Many of those examining the wreckage in the port at the close of 1941 were appalled. CINCPAC Adm. Chester W. Nimitz thought several of the sunken ships were finished. Despite the carnage, plans were made to raise as many of the ships as quickly as possible in an enterprise which, when completed, would prove one of the engineering "Miracles" of the Second World War.

As the new year 1942 dawned, efforts to get the *California* up were begun under the able general direction of Pearl Harbor Navy Yard salvage boss Capt. Homer N. Wallin, with Lt. W.L. Painter the "Prune Barge" project officer. They, together with the ship's Acting Captain, Cmdr. J.F. Warris, various divers and salvage experts, and all of the ship's ratings not yet transferred, quickly recognized one important fact—the slow sinking meant that the *California* was not badly damaged below the waterline. It was then decided to refloat the damaged port side. Using an untried idea, the seals on the subsequently-built patches would be made of tremic cement, the underwater kind used for bridges and drydocks. To make the refloating job easier, the first step would be to lighten the ship.

Warris and 500 bluejackets began the awesome task of clearing the *California*. Nine of the twelve 14-inch guns were removed (those in turret no. 4 were underwater and therefore unremovable), as were the broadside guns, the ship and flag towers, the catapults, cranes, boats, anchors and anchor chain, and the main mast, which was cut off at its base. Meanwhile, engineers and divers, mainly from the Pacific Bridge Company, built wooden fence-like cofferdams, which were placed around the quarterdeck and in the forecastle area. When huge deep-well centrifugal pumps arrived, and as divers plugged the leaks, the huge electrical machines, with power from Ford Island, pushed out thousands of gallons of water.

As the pumps gradually lowered the water level, workmen cleaned out the refuse compartment by compartment. Regular and canteen stores plus 14-inch and lesser shells and powder were removed. Personal property was put under guard and classified information was turned over to the proper authorities. About 200,000 gallons of free oil was collected. Meanwhile, Cmdr. Hyman G. Rickover became involved in a plan which could allow 50 G.E. specialists and over 100 Pearl Harbor electricians to reclaim and recondition the ship's various electrical motors and electric-drive machinery. Rotten stores were flushed out and with great dignity, a number of bodies were sent ashore for identification and burial. In a pleasant surprise, it was found that the work of plugging leaks was so successful that the overflow from the pumps was greater than the inflow of water. This good news meant that, with additional plugging, it would be possible to raise the dreadnought without patches over the torpedo damage.

The *California* came afloat almost on an even keel on March 24, 1942, her draft being about 40 feet. Once the cofferdams were struck off, she was placed in Drydock No.

2 on April 9, where she was welcomed by Adm. Nimitz, who had come down personally to witness the event. The *California* remained in dock until June 7. In the dock, permanent structural repairs were made to almost all of her damage. After a few trials to test her power and seaworthiness, Warris' vessel departed Pearl Harbor under her own power on October 10. A week later, she met the brand new destroyer *Gansevoort* (DD-608), and arrived at the Puget Sound Navy Yard on October 20.

Capt. Henry P. Burnett, who had assumed command in October 1943, began a rigid curruculum of standardization trials as soon as the newly-modernized "old battleship" (OBB) got under way for the first time on January 31, 1944. Taking her down the coast to San Pedro, the skipper oversaw gunnery and machinery tests, maneuvering and radar drills, conducted by the thousands of new officers and ratings, many draftees or reservists fresh from continental training stations. Seamanship drills, first aid and fire fighting lectures, and more gunnery were the order of the day, but in those first weeks, the newness of the crew caused many a drill to go awry. On May 5, after an engine check, she steamed to Pearl Harbor.

Mooring at "Fox 3," the same place in which she was savaged on December 7, 1941, the *California* was soon assigned to Fire Support Group One (Task Group 52.17), under Rear Adm. Jesse Oldendorf. After a week of intensive short bombardment rehearsals off Maui and Kahoolawe, Oldendorf's heavies departed Hawaiian waters for Kwajalein. At that central Pacific site, the ships would prepare for "Operation Forager," commanded by Vice Adm. Richard K. Turner. On June 10, 1944, the "Prune Barge" and her task group left Roi anchorage. All rumors as to the former flagship's destination ended when the executive officer, Cmdr. F.R. Bunker came on the PA with a message from the skipper. The ship's objective: Saipan Island in the Marianas.

Reveille sounded aboard the *California* an hour before dawn on June 14. Clothed in fresh garments, many men were at their stations before general quarters sounded. Rounding Saipan's northern tip as the sun rose, Burnett's vessel launched her float planes for air spotting and gingerly maneuvered into position off Garapan, the island's capital. With directors on target and the main batteries trained out, the standby buzzer went off in the turrets. Then, at precisely 0548, the *California's* high capacity (HC) bombardment shells began crashing home against the enemy batteries and supply dumps inland of the selected landing area—the southern portion of Saipan's west coast—in support of minesweepers carrying out an assault sweep of the landing zone. The *Maryland* (BB-46) drew fire from a concealed battery on a tiny islet off Tanapag harbor, but she, together with gunners on the *California* quickly put it out of business.

The *California* next provided cover for underwater demolition teams reconnoitering the landing area. As the *California* closed the beaches to within

The California *was back in the war in the spring of 1944 to join other ships the enemy thought it had destroyed during the Pearl Harbor attack.* NA #80-G-211831

3,000 yards to ply her 5-inch and 40mm projectiles, Japanese defenders began a murderous small arms and mortar attack on the frogmen. Heavier guns on nearby Tinian Island joined in and soon geysers were appearing in the water alongside the *California*. Then a shell from one of those concealed batteries hit on the dreadnought's upper deck aft, penetrating to explode. Damage control parties reacted quickly, and as the duel continued, crewmen learned that one of their comrades had been killed and 14 wounded. Late that afternoon after collecting the OS2U planes, the *California* took up her night station west of Saipan; there her officers and men could reflect on how this war had become such a "serious business" so quickly.

At 0430 June 15, the pre-landing bombardment of Saipan began. In a new target area off the town of Charon Kanoa, a tall sugar mill smokestack was chosen as a base sight in the *California's* preparatory softening of the beach. Her aerial spotters calling correction, salvo after salvo departed the big guns while tracers from her 40mm projectiles drifted into the beach to disappear in clouds of dust, blossoms of fire. Oldendorf's ships lifted their fire at 0630 for an air strike and then recommenced until, with the 2nd and 4th Marine Division landing craft within a thousand yards of the beach at 0812, the three flares of the cease fire signal appeared in the air. The naval bombard-

Somewhere in the Pacific, 1944.

USN (All Hands)

The California *in the floating drydock at Espirtu Santo, New Hebrides getting repairs from the collision with the* Tennessee*, August 1944.* USN

ment had proved to be less than a total success and many Japanese positions were not damaged; the leathernecks would face extremely tough going.

Connonading became a routine call fire pastime for the *California* during the remainder of the Saipan operation; one sailor called the practice "a Navy-sponsored farm project that simultaneously plows the fields, prunes the trees, harvests the crops, and adds iron to the soil." There was one night of excitement, however, which should have broken the routine.

On the evening of June 16, the Japanese 136th Infantry Regiment as part of a general counteroffensive and backed up by armor of the 9th Tank Regiment, moved against the positions of the 6th Marines. This, the first sizeable Japanese tank attack of the Pacific island fighting, brought emergency calls to the "duty ship" *California*. Firing both star and explosive shells, Burnett's gunners helped the Marines turn back determined enemy charges which left 700 enemy soldiers dead and 31 light/medium

tanks knocked out.

As part of the plan which brought the Japanese tanks into the *California's* range, Japanese admirals attempted a naval relief of the Marianas. Departing the beaches at daylight on June 17, the *California* joined Oldendorf's task group in patrolling west of Saipan. Over the next three days, planes from Task Force 58 wiped out the Imperial naval air force in what American carrier men later called the "Marianas Turkey Shoot." Released, the *California* retired to Eniwetok where her battle damage of June 14 was repaired by mid-July.

At Guam on July 19, the *California* and her sister, the *Tennessee*, took up their labors as the heavy fire support units in Rear Adm. Richard Connolly's Southern Attack Force. From early on July 20 until 0830 the following morning, the two Pearl Harbor veterans assisted in the pre-invasion pounding of the island's northwest coast. Late on July 21 after the Marines were ashore, the sisters returned to Saipan to rejoin TG 52.17.

Bow view in the floating drydock, August 1944.

USN

Tinian is separated by a three-mile channel from Saipan. On July 23, the *California* and *Tennessee*, directed by Rear Adm. Howard F. Kingman, bombarded coastal defenses near Tinian Town as a diversion for the main landing further north. After the leathernecks hit the beach, the two ships alternated call fire duty through the remainder of the month as Marines and warships pushed the Japanese toward annihilation on the high ground of the island's southern tip. On July 31, the *California's* guns fell silent as a command message came aboard: "Your mission completed. Proceed anchorage. Sorry we could not find more targets for you." The *California* and *Tennessee* were almost immediately switched back into the Guam fight, where they provided fire from August 2-8 before anchoring at Eniwetok on the 9th.

Three days later, the sister dreadnoughts joined a small task force steaming for Espiritu Santo, New Hebrides. With the men on the ships anticipating a well-earned bit of rest and relaxation, "pollywogs" by the hundreds were initiated "into the deep in the salty presence of King Neptune and his royal party" in the traditional equator-crossing ceremonies, held on August 21.

Just before reveille on the 23rd, however, *California's* crew received a rude awakening. Wildly out of control due to a steering malfunction, *Tennessee* smashed her stem into *California's* port bow, tearing a large gash forward of 14-inch turret I. Though the collision pierced several compartments, opening them to the sea, injuries were few. With all trapped sailors rescued, and all damage sealed, the "Prune Barge" returned to convoy, her men looking forward to shore leave more than ever.

In a record 17-day period, August 25-September 10, the *California's* collision repairs were effected in Espiritu Santo's floating drydock. Departing the New Hebrides on September 17, Burnett's vessel slipped up the New Guinea coast to Seeadler Harbor, Manus, in the Admiralties, arriving four days later. Here she was assigned to that half of the Bombardment and Fire Support Group destined to support a Southern Attack Force, U.S. 7th Fleet. The time had come to redeem General MacArthur's famous pledge to the people of the Philippines: "I Shall Return."

On October 17, 1944, after a five-day voyage, the *California* and *Tennessee* arrived off Leyte Gulf. Following preliminary minesweeping, the sisters, streaming paravanes to cut cables of missed mines, and followed by the *West Virginia* (BB-48), themselves followed the flagship *Pennsylvania* (BB-38) inside the gulf through a marked channel. Around sundown, the starboard paravane of the "Prune Barge" cut loose a mine which bobbed to the surface and bore down on the "WeeVee," which successfully dodged it at the last minute.

The ships took up their positions off Dulag before sunrise on October 19 and at 0645 began to bombard the designated landing area south of the town, a shoot which continued throughout the day. After additional post-dawn softening, American soldiers returned to the Philippines at 1000 on October 20. The landings went well and soon the *California* was shifting her fire inland and to the flanks to assist the troops as they began carving out a beachhead.

As the Leyte invasion unfolded, the Japanese decided to strike back and sent four widely-separated forces to destroy the American operation. In an effort to join a larger fleet in a pincer movement against the 7th Fleet amphibious ships and transports, Vice Adm. Shoji Nishimura led the 30-year old 14-inch battleship *Fuso* and

Yamishiro, the cruiser *Mogami*, and four destroyers toward Surigao Strait. Alerted by Navy reconnaissance, Adm. Oldendorf sought to deal with the situation by placing his six old battleships, eight cruisers, and 28 destroyers across the northern end of that passage late on October 24.

After securing from anti-aircraft defense that evening, off-duty *California* crewmen went below to get as much sleep as possible, although several preferred to stretch out and nap on the cooler upper decks. Others watched as the ship took on oil; armorers checked the magazine and firehoses were faked out and unnecessary gear was secured—or tossed overboard. Fire control instruments received a thorough check as radar and radio technicians made certain that secondary stations could be rigged quickly if the need arose. Other sailors lugged water, blankets, and C-rations to their stations while a crew, after watching the Kingfishers fly off to the beach, lowered the catapult crane. Below, medical personnel saw to the sick bay's readiness. All anxiously awaited the ship's first surface action.

Moving out in line, the battlewagons patrolled the moonless night, moving back and forth across the smooth sea, which nevertheless featured a strong current, difficult for helmsmen. GQ was sounded aboard the *California* at 0130. All battle stations were fully manned and alert, ammunition was readied for instant loading, and the ship's watertight integrity made as secure as possible. Lookouts peering into the dark could make out the other members of the Pearl Harbor "survivor's association," but those below and inside the turrets could see nothing.

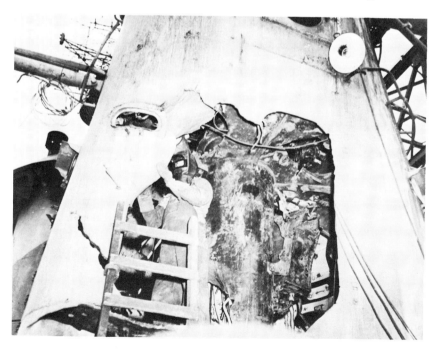

Repairing battle damage received in Lingayen Gulf, January 1945.   USN

Photos showing action in Lingayen Gulf, Philippines, January 1945. The California *was hit by a Kamikaze in its after fire control tower.*　　　All Photos USN

Beginning his thrust up the straight, Adm. Nishimura was soon found out. At 2236 that October 25, U.S. PT boats deployed in the passage made radar contact and, followed by destroyers, they attacked, causing the enemy ships much damage and confusion. *California* observers could see the distant flashes of gunfire, searchlight, and star shells which marked the engagement. Just after 0300, the battlewagon's radar picked up the Japanese approach at nearly 44,000 yards and began tracking the lead ship *Yamashiro*. *Yamishiro*, the cruiser, and one destroyer were all that had made it past the lighter American forces and the three were now acting like the cavalry in the "Charge of the Light Brigade." As Nishimura pushed further into this "valley of death," his success probability was reduced to zero.

Steadily the distance shrank and at 0355, after the *West Virginia* had received the honor of opening fire, Capt. Burnett was granted permission to commence firing: the range was point-blank, 20,500 yards. In the brief battle which followed, the *California*, *Tennessee*, and *West Virginia*, owing to their new gunfire radar and instruments, got off most of the telling shots. Firing in six-gun salvoes to consume a precious and limited supply of anti-personnel shells, the *California* poured 63 rounds of 14-inch shells at the enemy. Only 16 minutes after the first salvo, Burnett ceased firing. Surigao Straight did much to avenge his ship's loss at Pearl Harbor; of all Nishimura's ships committed to the "charge," only the destroyer *Shigure* escaped.

Following several weeks off Leyte, the *California* was released to the New Hebrides. There, in late November 1944, Capt. Samuel B. Brewer succeeded Capt. Burnett as skipper. On December 19, Brewer took his new command into Kossol Passage, the Palaus, there to celebrate Christmas and prepare for yet another campaign.

The "return" to the Philippines continued apace into the new year 1945. On New Year's Day and with Adm. Oldendorf embarked, the *California* quit the Palaus and, as flagship of TG 77.2, led an armada of vessels through Leyte Gulf and the Sulu Sea to the northwest coast of Luzon. Resistance was stiff from enemy warplanes along the route, especially from a new band of suicide flyers known as Kamikazes. On January 5, Oldendorf's ships reached Lingayen Gulf and early the next morning, preliminary minesweeping was completed. As gunners watched the skies, the "Prune Barge," keeping fresh, pounded targets on Santiago Island on the western side of Lingayen's entrance. After lunch, the flagship led a great gray column of fire support vessels into Lingayen Gulf to attack targets in and around the designated invasion area.

Adm. Oldendorf's fleet met determined opposition from Japan's air arm and soon most of his ships' gunners were in action. As the flagship was gliding toward her assigned bombardment position, she, too, became the target of a Kamikaze. Coming in low over the bow of a nearby destroyer, a "Zero" fighter sped toward the *California's* bridge. Smoke from anti-aircraft guns blanketed the battleship's starboard side as gunners and loaders swung with the plane. The blizzard of fire was, however, to no avail; the pilot flipped his plane into a vertical bank and ripped into the after fire control tower. Violent yellow flames billowed as the ship rocked with the explosion. Meteoric shell fragments tore chunks out of the deck 35 feet below, demolished gun stations, smashed splinter shields, and even bit into the ship's bell. Damage control parties worked quickly and methodically and within 12 minutes, all fires were extinguished. Of the 203 casualties incurred in the disaster, six officers and 26

men were killed outright with 13 later succumbing to injuries; 155 officers and hands were wounded while three crewmen were reported missing. Temporarily repaired while under way, the *California* hammered Luzon positions on January 7-9, as troops went ashore on the 9th. She remained on station providing call fire support unfil January 22, when she departed for Bremerton, via Ulithi and Pearl Harbor.

Workmen at the Puget Sound Navy Yard repaired the *California's* damage and after training exercises for the many new men, the OBB returned to the fray, anchoring at Hagushi Bay, Okinawa, on June 15. By now, the worst was over in the great final land-sea-air battle. Ashore, Army troops made a finishing drive to clear the island; gunfire from the *California* helped snuff out a few remaining pockets of resistance. With the other old dreadnoughts, she remained ready in support until the campaign was declared over on June 21.

On July 22, the *California* joined Task Force 95; with Oldendorf's group, the old lady covered minesweeping operations in the East China Sea and patrolled the waters off Shanghai for Japanese shipping as escort carriers sent strikes against the China coast. Aside from an August visit to the Philippines, this was the ship's duty until V-J Day brought an end to the war in the Pacific.

In the Surigao Strait, January 1945.

USN #N-3155A

37

The battlewagon's final assignment of World War II was to cover the landing of 6th Army occupation troops at Wakanoura Wan, on the island of Honshu. With the *Tennessee*, she arrived in Japan on September 23; then, on October 3, the two sisters moved to Yokosuka, where the *California* berthed near the wreckage of the once-proud dreadnought *Negato*. Crewmen had the chance to look over the erstwhile Imperial Navy's big base and do some sightseeing before their group got under way for Singapore a dozen days later. During the Japanese lull, Capt. Brewer was succeeded by Capt. Lunsford Y. Mason, Jr. From Singapore, the *California* and her sister continued their long voyage, via Colombo and Capetown. Finally, after 15,000 miles, they moored in the Philadelphia Navy Yard on December 7, the fourth anniversary of Pearl Harbor.

The *California* earned six battle stars during her wartime career for participation in the following operations:

1. Pearl Harbor-Midway   7 December 1941
2. Marianas Operation
     Capture and occupation of Saipan   14 June 1944-20 June 1944
     Capture and occupation of Tinian   21 July 1944-2 August 1944
     Capture and occupation of Guam   2 August 1944-9 August 1944
3. Leyte Operation
     Leyte Landings   21 November 1944
4. Luzon Operation
     Lingayen Gulf Landing   4 January 1945-18 January 1945
5. Okinawa-Gunto Operation
     Assault and occupation of   17 June 1945-30 June 1945
     Okinawa-Gunto
6. Third Fleet Operations Against Japan   10 July 1945-7 August 1945

The process of trimming the Navy down to postwar size required that older, yet useful, ships be assigned to "mothballs." By summer 1946, the *California's* last skipper, Cmdr. Forrest M. Price, who had succeeded Capt. Mason in March, had preservation work well in hand. On August 7, the ship was placed in commission in reserve. Seven months later, on February 14, 1947, after guns and machinery were rust- and water-proofed, the ensign of the "Prune Barge" was hauled down for the last time as she was placed out of commission.

The *California* remained in the inactive reserve fleet for another twelve years. By then, time and technology had passed her by and, on March 1, 1959, her name was stricken from the Naval Vessel Register. On March 1 of that year, she was sold for scrap to the Boston Metals Company, Baltimore, Maryland for $860,000. The veteran battlewagon arrived at the head of Chesapeake Bay the following March under tow. There, after a few mementos were saved, she was completely broken up by the end of summer, 1960.

Wartime photo.   USN

The California docked at Capetown, South Africa, on her 15,000 mile trip from the Pacific to Philadelphia after the war was over. NA #80-G-374360

The battleship edges into port at Philadelphia, Pa., after the war was over. She was scheduled for inactive duty. USN (All Hands)

THE NUCLEAR GUIDED MISSILE CRUISER
CALIFORNIA (CGN-36)

The advantages of an all-nuclear carrier task force were demonstrated in 1964 when, in "Operation Sea Orbit," the *USS Enterprise* (CVAN-65), *Long Beach* (CGN-9), and *Bainbridge* (DLGN-25) circled the globe at full speed and without replenishment in only 65 days. When the nuclear carrier *Nimitz* (CVAN-68) was authorized in FY 1967, two nuclear-powered escorts were also approved, the lead ship to be named *California*. Developed from the *Bainbridge*, the new ship, originally classified as a nuclear-powered guided missile frigate, would prove to be a larger and more sophisticated warship, distinguishable from the earlier DLGN by her flush deck and enclosed masts. Indeed, without big-gun turrets or stacks, but possessed of pylon mast supports, a box-like superstructure, and tall, enclosed towers supporting radar antennae, the *California* can be said to typify the "new Navy" which emerged in the years after World War II. In recognition of these differences, the Golden State namesake was reclassified as a nuclear-powered guided missile cruiser on June 30, 1975.

The contract for the sixth and most powerful *California* was awarded to the Newport News Shipbuilding and Drydock Company in June 1968 and her keel laid on January 23, 1970. Twenty-two months later on September 22, 1971, she was launched, sponsored by First Lady Patricia Nixon. Outfitting lagged, but the new Golden State representative was finally commissioned on February 16, 1974, Capt. Floyd H. Miller, Jr., commanding. Her cost has been estimated as being between $200 million and $220 million—more than the total cost of her five predecessors combined. This tremendous figure, when coupled with the development of the even more advanced CGN-38 *(Virginia)* class, caused a third ship of this group to be cancelled. The *California* and *South Carolina* (CGN-37) would be one of the smallest purpose-built classes of warships built for the Navy after the Second World War.

The Golden State cruiser's principal function is that of carrier escort. Consequently, her design and armament are primarily those associated with task force ASW and anti-aircraft work, although she can function in more specialized groups even to the point of shore bombardment. Her aluminum and metal hull is painted gray and displays her hull numbers prominently on the bow, with smaller numbers and her name in painted raised letters at the stern. This advanced combatant displaces 9,561 tons (normal) and 11,100 tons (full load). She is 596 feet long (only 4 feet short of the waterline length of BB-44) with a beam of 61 feet and a draft of 31 feet 6 inches. Berths are provided for 28 officers and 512 men.

A pair of pressurized, water-cooled D2G General Electric nuclear reactors, each with $11.5 million cores, provide the steam to power two geared turbines and other machinery infinitely more sophisticated than that aboard the "electric drive" battleship which was her state predecessor. A decade of normal ship operations (or 700,000 miles) was estimated before refueling would be necessary. The *California's*

engines provide 60,000 S.H.P. (compared to BB-44's 28,500) and can drive her two propellers at a speed in excess of 30 knots.

The cruiser's primary ASW weaponry is ASROC; an eight-tube launcher is located just forward of the bridge. Four tubes for MK 32 torpedoes are sited aft while echo-ranging is provided by an SQS-26CX bow-mounted sonar. A MK 114 underwater battery fire control system is also onboard. Although a landing pad is located at the stern for both conventional and LAMPS helicopters, no maintenance facilities are provided as "choppers" could normally be expected to operate from an accompanying carrier.

The *California's* primary anti-aircraft armament consists of two single Tartar-D twin-missile launchers mounted well forward and aft. These fire the MK 13, Mod 3 Standard medium-range (MR) surface-to-air missile, about 40 of which are held in magazines below each launcher. Plans call for the ship to be refitted (if it has not already been) with Standard SR-2's. This anti-aircraft weaponry is controlled by a pair of MK 74, Mod 4 fire control systems, with four fore and aft mounted SPG-51 radars. To deal with low-flying aircraft, fast patrol boats, or shore targets, the cruiser has two 5-inch/54 caliber dual purpose guns mounted in single automatic turrets, one forward between the ASROC and Tartar-D launchers and one on the "02" deck portion of the after superstructure. These are controlled by a MK 86, Mod 3 fire control system for which there is also an SPG-60 radar. Two 40mm saluting guns are carried and when they become available, a pair of MK 15 20mm Phalanx close-in weapons systems (CIWS), each with six-barrel Vulcan "gatling guns," will be mounted for last-ditch defense against antiship (SSM) missiles. Additionally in a move designed to exert her offensive range and capability, the installation of Harpoon SSM's is imminent. The *California* is equipped with SPS-10 and SPS-40 sear radar with an SPS-48 3-D radar on the foremast. Her communications gear features an SSR-1 receiver, a WSC-3 transceiver, and an OE-82 satellite communications antenna. These various systems are supported by a three-computer Naval Tactical Data System (NTDS) complex.

With her home port at Norfolk, the *California* has been in service for almost a decade now. In those years, she has sailed to far seas on a variety of missions, mostly routine carrier escort deployments. The service, just as hard and enjoyable for today's sailors as it was for those who manned earlier Golden State warships, has brought pride to her crew and participation in a few memorable events.

In 1977, the *California* was the only American representative in the multi-nation naval review held to honor the Silver Jubilee of Britain's Queen Elizabeth. In 1979-1980, the ship participated in the screen of U.S. warships sent to the Indian Ocean in response to the Iran hostage crisis. On November 20, 1981, after what had begun as a routine deployment to the Indian Ocean, Capt. Charles J. Smith brought

The Nuclear Powered Guided Missile Frigate USS California *(DLGN-36) off the Virginia Capes, May 1975.*

USN #K-108976

his command back to Hampton Roads. After steaming 78,000 miles, the Golden State cruiser had become the first Navy vessel in years to circumnavigate the earth.

For seven months, Smith's ship had spent most of its time under way. In the Indian Ocean on July 15, 1981, the *California* was detached from the *America* (CVA-66) battle group to rescue 39 seamen from the fatally-stricken Greek merchantman *Irenes Sincerity*. As the cruiser continued her voyage, she would become involved in two more at-sea rescues, saving a man from a deserted island and picking up four downed helicopter crewmen. This globe-circling mission was taxing in some respects; only 19 days liberty were allowed, 16 accounted for by calls at Cartagena, Spain; Singapore; and Perth, Australia. The other three days came in San

Diego on the final leg of the trek home.

As the *California* entered the port of San Diego, she was met and escorted by fire boats and a flotilla of pleasure craft, many carrying veterans of the old "Prune Barge," BB-44. An airborne banner, arranged for by local Navy League members, proclaimed the city's welcome. The ship's crew was officially welcomed; the celebration marked the first time that the cruiser had visited the state for which she was named. "We've had many invitations to visit various cities in California," said Capt. Smith, "and we finally made it." When the latest Golden State namesake departed San Diego for home and future missions, there were a few tears, many smiles, and hopes that she would make it again one day soon.

Launching ceremony of DLGN-36 at the Newport News Shipbuilding and Dry Dock Company, Sept. 22, 1971. USN #1149458

DLGN-36 backs into a pier at Norfolk, Va., 1981. USN (All Hands)

Model of the California *(BB-44) on display at the National Maritime Museum, Golden Gate National Recreation Area, San Francisco, Calif. It was built in 1922 by Uno T. Ovlen at the Mare Island Navy Yard. It is built to be a one-quarter scale and is 13 feet long and 2 feet and 1-3/16 inches wide.* National Maritime Museum

Bell of the USS California *(BB-44) on the grounds of the California State Capitol, Sacramento.* Ray Carter, Sacramento, Calif.

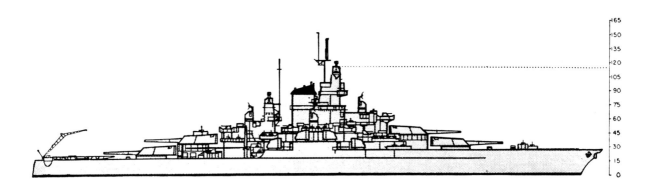

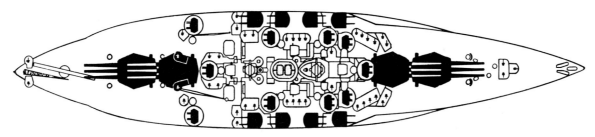

BB—Battleships—TENNESSEE Class

BB 43—TENNESSEE

Completed—June 1920
Modernized—1942

BB 44—CALIFORNIA

Completed—August 1921
Modernized—1943

Dimensions

Displacement:
   32,300 tons (stand) (TENN.)
   32,600 tons (stand) (CALIF.)
   40,400 tons (Mean War Service)
Length: 624′ (oa)
Beam: 114′
Draft: 34′ (max)

Armament

12 14″/50
16 5″/38 DP
10 40 mm quads
43–60 20 mm

Propulsion

Speed: 19 knots (max)
Max. cruising radius:
   6,400 miles @ 19 knots
   9,200 miles @ 15 knots
Horsepower: 29,000 (shaft)
Drive: 4 screws; turbo-electric
Fuel: 4,893 tons oil (max)

Aircraft

2 SC–1